CHO-CHO and THE HEALTH FAIRY Six Stories

Nadakkavu, Kozhikode, Kerala, 673011
www.insightpublica.com
e-mail: insightpublica@gmail.com

Title: **CHO-CHO and THE HEALTH FAIRY Six Stories**
Author: **ELEANOR GLENDOWER GRIFFITH**
First Insight Edition: August 2024
Copyright © Reserved
All rights reserved.
Printed and Published by
InsightinPublica Printers & Publishers Pvt. Ltd.
ISBN 9789355176745

CHO-CHO and THE HEALTH FAIRY Six Stories

ELEANOR GLENDOWER GRIFFITH

contents

The House the Children Built

Once upon a time there lived a good and beautiful Fairy named Health, and she was very happy, for all around were flowers and trees and birds and in the midst of these, her house.

Now Health's house was built of bricks and shingles and lovely colored glass. One day when the sky was blue and the sun shining, down the road came an ugly old Witch. Her face was hard and her eyes were very cruel. She stopped in front of Health's lovely garden and from her pocket drew forth a yellow ball and threw it with all her strength toward the house.

It settled on the roof, and where it fell there sprang forth fire, which spread and spread over the house, until it was a mass of flames. Fairy Health ran to the well for water, but before her tiny hands could draw the water up from the well, her house was burnt beyond all help.

When the Witch, whose name was Ignorance, saw the harm she had done, she laughed a cruel laugh and hobbled down the road.

Poor little Fairy Health sank upon the grass in her garden and cried. At last she was conscious of a voice and looking up, saw in a green bush quite near a lovely Bird, who said: 6"Keep up your courage, Fairy, for I will tell you how to build your house anew."

Health dried her eyes upon a sweet geranium leaf, and asked him how that could possibly be done.

The Bird replied: "It can be done by the hands of Children alone. Every time a Child learns to eat the right food, a brick shall be added to your house, every time a Child learns to sleep in the sweet fresh air, a shingle shall be put upon the roof. And every time a Child learns to play and be happy, a colored glass shall be added to the windows."

"But alas!" said Fairy Health, "How shall we teach the Children these things?"

"I will go to the Teachers who are wise and good," said the Bird, "and tell them what to do."

So the Bird, whose name was Education, started on his journey. He took his brother Rumor with him to help tell the Teachers, because there were a great many Teachers to be told about the Children's health.

Far and near these wise birds traveled, to little towns and to big cities, and everywhere the Teachers listened to their story, until in all that great country, the Children were taught to eat wholesome food, to sleep in the sweet fresh air, and to play and be happy.

And as the Children grew healthy and happy, the bricks were added to the Fairy's house, and shingles were put upon the roof. Lovely colored glass filled up the broken 7windows, and once again there stood among the trees and flowers a house so beautiful that strangers, passing by, paused to admire it. Health often invited them to rest in her garden, and as she refreshed them with sparkling water from the well, she told the story of her house, and how Children had rebuilt it for her.

What is that,
O powerful Witch.

The Magic Oat Field

One day as the Fairy Health sat within her Rose Arbor, there came walking down the road a tiny Elf. He had a merry face and a bright smile, and pausing beside the Garden Gate, he asked:

"Does Health live here?"

"I am Health," said the Fairy, and rose to greet him. The Elf drew from his pocket a little card, on which was written "Cho-Cho, the Friend of Children," and presented it to the Fairy.

"I come," he said, "to view the wonders of your Garden, and to learn from you the secrets of a Child's Heart."

The good Fairy took Cho-Cho's hand and leading him by many lovely paths, came at length into a Field of ripening Oats. On the borders of the Field grew flowers of many colors, and the air was filled with perfume.

Health paused and said: "As long as these beautiful Oats flourish I know that everywhere in all this great country Children can eat Oatmeal for their breakfast and grow strong and healthy, but if the Oats should wither and die, something dreadful would happen to the Children."

Even as she spoke, a strange light settled on the Oat Field, and the beautiful waving grain began to shrivel and wither away.

10A look of terror came into the Fairy's eyes. As Cho-Cho turned to clasp her hand in sympathy, suddenly there stood beside him a handsome Persian Cat.

"Don't lose heart, little Fairy," said Puss, "I will help you. Last night, as I was walking in the moonlight, I saw an ugly old Witch creep into your garden.

"In her hand she carried a large strong box. I hid behind a bush and saw her open the box. As she raised the lid, out sprang swarms of tiny insects and flew toward the Oat Field. The Witch laughed a harsh laugh, and said, 'Go, little imps— work quickly, for your time is short.'

"I understand magic, Fairy, and can change at will into any shape that pleases me—so in the twinkling of an eye I became a Witch too, and walking slowly forward, I said, 'A fine night, Madam Witch. What do you here?'

"The old Witch jumped when she heard my voice, but seeing it was only a Witch like herself, she grinned horribly and said: 'I have persuaded hundreds of children to stop eating Oatmeal, and every time a Child refuses Oatmeal, one of these little imps is born. Before tomorrow night the Fairy's Oat Field will be withered and dead. One thing only can stop these imps of mine,' she chuckled.

"'What is that, O powerful Witch?' I asked.

"'I must be bound fast with chains of steel. If such a thing could happen my imps would quickly die and the Children would eat Oatmeal again and the Field regain its beauty, but ha! ha! no one can bind me.'

11"'You must be very clever, Madam Witch,' I said, 'But it grows late and I must away.'

"So I left her there and went to my home."

"What shall I do?" the little Fairy cried. "What shall I do?"

"Be not discouraged, Fairy," said the Persian Cat, "I am your friend, follow me."

Down the road the cat led them for fully half a mile, until they came to a forest of fir trees. Quiet reigned within the wood. It was so very still that even their soft footsteps on the pine needles could be heard. There was no light except from far above their heads, where the blue sky shone through the green branches of the trees.

Puss went on and on, until Cho-Cho and the Fairy were growing quite tired. At last he stopped before a huge tree whose branches touched the ground. Parting these, the Cat entered, and followed by his two friends, stood beside the Tree.

"Wonderful, Wonderful, Wonderful Tree,

Open, Oh open your door unto me!"

Slowly the trunk of the great Tree opened and they beheld a narrow stairway leading down, down, farther than their eyes could see.

"Come," said the Cat, "the Witch lives here. Step lightly or we may rouse her."

12Softly, very softly, they crept down those narrow steps, until at last they entered a dark room. Its only light came from a fire of coals, and before this fire the Witch lay sleeping. Springing upon her, Puss bound her arms and feet with chains of steel, and she lay helpless before them, uttering cries of hate and wickedness.

"Wonderful Cat, who are you?" said Cho-Cho.

"I am Knowledge," said the Cat, "and this cruel Witch is Ignorance, who spends her life plotting against the health of Children. Between us there is always war. Lie there, Ignorance, while the Children you wish to kill grow strong and healthy. Fairy, your Oat Field is beautiful again."

Leaving the dark home of Ignorance, they traveled through the sweet scented forest, back to the garden of the Fairy Health. There they found that the Cat had told them true, for the Oat Field was beautiful beyond words. The blue sky smiled above, and the summer wind blew over it, carrying the perfume of a thousand flowers, and all the world seemed full of peace.

"Cat, dear Cat, what can we do for you?" said Cho-Cho.

"Only this," said Puss, "help me to fight Ignorance."

From his finger the Cat took two tiny rings. One he gave to Cho-Cho and one to the Fairy.

"If ever again this cruel Witch arises to destroy the Children's Oatmeal, turn this ring upon your finger twice and say:

"Knowledge, Knowledge,

Wherever you be,

Come, Oh, come,

The Children need Thee!"

And as he said this, Puss waved a gay "Good-bye" and walked gracefully away.

He saw a little boy
thin and pale.

The Wonderful Window

Cho-Cho, a tiny Elf, built his house upon the roof of a tall office building in a great city. He chose a sunny corner of the chimney, and there with sticks and strings, brought to him by his friends, the Sparrows, he erected a cozy little Home.

On the outside, it was quite pretty, but after you entered the door and saw the fire on the hearth, and Cho-Cho's armchair and books beside it, you decided that it was the most charming little house in all that noisy city.

Now within this house was a Magic Window, and from this window Cho-Cho could look into all the homes where Children lived.

Sitting beside the Magic Window one day, Cho-Cho beheld a sight that filled his heart with pity. In a dingy room he saw a thin, pale little Boy, sitting beside a rough table, on which the only food was some cheap buns and coffee. As Cho-Cho looked, he saw the Child try to raise the heavy cup to his lips, but his little hands were far too weak, and it fell with a crash upon the floor, breaking into many pieces, and spilling the coffee. Now this Child loved coffee, because all his life he had been used to drinking it. As he saw the coffee wasted on the floor, he laid his head upon the table and cried and cried and cried. Presently he fell asleep.

As he slept, Cho-Cho stood beside him, and taking his 16hand, led him far, far away from the great city and all its noise and danger. When the little Boy woke, he was walking down a quiet country road and Cho-Cho was with him. Wild grass and violets grew along this road, and far away on either side stretched fields of lovely clover, whose pink blossoms swayed in the wind.

Passing through a gateway, they entered the field. And now they saw an old farm house surrounded by trees. In the door stood a Sweet-faced Woman, who looked at them with kindly interest.

"Lady," said Cho-Cho, "this little Boy has no Mother. Will you give him a glass of your good milk? He is very faint."

Then a strange thing happened. Cho-Cho vanished. He had been standing right beside the little Boy and then suddenly he was gone.

The little Boy began to cry, and the Farmer's Wife, whose heart was full of love for children, and who had none of her own, gathered him up in her strong arms, and carried him into the large kitchen.

Here she gave him fresh Brown Bread to eat and Milk that was sweet and cool, and he ate and ate, until he could eat no more.

As the days went by, the good Woman learned to love the little Boy as if he were her own, and he grew so strong and healthy that no one would have imagined him the same 17lonely Child that Cho-Cho had brought to the Farm House. All day long he played in the sweet clover-scented

   CHO-CHO and THE HEALTH FAIRY Six

air, sometimes with the little calves in the field, but more often beside the Dairy, where the Sweet-faced Woman spent so much of her time.

The Dairy was built of stone, and the walls were thick and deep. A little stream ran through it, and in a stone trough stood great crocks of Milk, Milk to make Children strong and healthy, for nothing in all the world is so good for Children as Milk. The stream sang among the Milk crocks, and the little Boy played beside the Dairy, and the good Woman smiled and was happy.

Then, one day while the little Boy was playing in the clover field, down the road came an old Witch. She smiled at the Child, and spoke pleasantly to him, but in her heart was hate and ugliness.

"Come walk with me, my dear," she said, "and I will give you coffee to drink."

The Farmer's Wife had often told the little Boy never to drink coffee for it was very bad for Children, but he liked coffee, so he took the old Witch's hand and followed her far, far away.

As the sunlight faded from the fields, and night came on, the Sweet-faced Woman missed the little Boy, and anxiously looked for him, but nowhere could he be found.

Now Cho-Cho from his Magic Window in the great city 18had never ceased to look each day toward the country and the Farm where the Boy lived, and as he saw the Child grow strong and healthy, he smiled with pleasure, for Cho-Cho was the Friend of Children.

But today as he looked, to his great surprise, he saw the Sweet-faced Woman sobbing on her doorstep, and he knew that something must be wrong. After putting out the living-room fire and locking the door of his house, Cho-Cho started at once for the Farm. The Woman still sat on her doorstep, sad with weeping.

"Lady," said Cho-Cho, "tell me your trouble."

Then she told him that the little Boy was lost.

"I will find him," said Cho-Cho, "for I have in my pocket a Magic Magnet, and when I hold it in my right hand, it will draw me toward anyone whom I wish to seek. Have courage, I will bring back your little Boy."

As he spoke, Cho-Cho drew out the Magic Magnet and held it in his right hand. Slowly the Magnet turned toward the sunny road, and Cho-Cho walked on.

The path was very rough and full of sharp stones, and ended at last in front of an enormous rock. In this rock was an iron door, so stout and heavy that it could not be opened, unless one had the key, and Cho-Cho had no key.

As Cho-Cho rested for a bit, feeling rather discouraged, he heard a voice, and there sat a Red Brown Squirrel.

19"What is wrong, Friend?" said the Squirrel.

"A little Boy is lost," said Cho-Cho, "and I know that he is behind this wall, but I cannot open the door."

"I can help you," said the Squirrel. Stooping, he picked up a small stone, and began to rub it between his paws. As he rubbed, the stone turned to iron, and quickly into a key that fitted the lock on the huge door.

"I thank you," said Cho-Cho. "What is your name?"

"I am Friendship," said the Squirrel, "and I will go with you on your journey."

Through the great door they went, and on again up the mountain, coming at last to the top, and there on the ground lay the little Boy. His clothes were soiled, and torn in many places, for the Witch had dragged him up the mountainside by one small arm, and the rough stones and briars had caught his garments as she hurried him onward. He was asleep where the Witch had thrown him. Cho-Cho's heart filled with pity when he saw the little figure lying there. Bending over, Cho-Cho gently touched the tear-stained face and the little Boy awoke.

"Where is the Witch?" Cho-Cho asked. The little Boy caught his hand in a frightened grasp. He was so afraid that he could scarcely speak.

"Cho-Cho, take me home," he sobbed, "take me home, before the Witch comes back."

20"She shall not hurt you," Cho-Cho answered. "But where did she go?"

Before the Child could speak, a harsh laugh sounded in their ears, a heavy stone whistled through the air, and fell beside Cho-Cho, barely missing his head, then all was very still.

"Stay with the Boy," Cho-Cho told the friendly Squirrel, "this Witch shall be punished."

The Magnet in his hand pointed directly toward a large rock. Its steep sides were very sharp and rough, and looking up Cho-Cho saw the ugly Witch standing on the top.

"So I am to be punished, am I?" she screamed, her face distorted by rage, "I will show you who has power here," and she hurled a sharp stone at Cho-Cho. Springing aside, Cho-Cho drew an arrow from its quiver and a stout bow from his back, and carefully aiming, he pulled the bow string. The arrow sped through the air, and struck the Witch with such force that she fell forward, and losing her balance, rolled over and over down the side of the great rock. When Cho-Cho reached the place where she lay unconscious, one arm hung limp at her side, broken by the fall. Her feet were scarred by heavy chains that had once bound her, and looking on her cruel face Cho-Cho said, "She has been punished enough."

Then taking the little Boy's hand, Cho-Cho started back to the Farm House. The Sweet-faced Woman met them on 21the road and when she saw the little Boy, her face lit up with happiness and love.

"What can I do for you, Cho-Cho?" she asked.

"Help little Children," Cho-Cho answered, and looking at his wrist watch, he saw it was quite late, and remembering a business engagement in the city, he hurried away.

Will you take me
on your back ?

The Little Vegetable Men

One sunny summer day, the little Fairy Health worked among her flowers, weeding and digging the rich brown earth to make them beautiful. She sang, as she worked, a gay little song, and tripped lightly here and there over the grass and flower beds. Stopping at last to wipe the earth from her hands upon a large lily leaf, for it made a most convenient towel, she looked up and saw Cho-Cho coming down the road and ran to the gate to greet him.

Now Cho-Cho was a tiny Elf who loved Children, and he was one of the Fairy's oldest friends.

"Fairy," said Cho-Cho, "in looking from my Magic Window last evening I saw the old Witch Ignorance abroad. Up and down the city streets she went and into all the homes where Children live, and on the door of every house she made a black mark."

"Oh, Cho-Cho," said the Fairy, "this means trouble for the Children."

"Yes," said Cho-Cho.

Leading him to a seat within her Rose Arbor, the Fairy brought him sparkling water from her well and bade him rest until he felt refreshed.

As she spoke, through the garden gate came three queer-looking little Men. The first had the head of a Beet, and 24his clothes were made from dull green leaves. His shoes and stockings were beet-colored and in his hand he carried a green hat.

The second little Man was a white Onion, and his clothes were the green of onion tops; and the third little fellow had the face of a Carrot, and he, too, was all in green.

"Fairy," said the little Man who looked like a Beet, "we are in great trouble and have come to ask for your help. We are called the Green Vegetables and are a large and happy family. Last night while we slept, the wicked Witch Ignorance crept in among us and carried off one of our little Men. We did not know that he was gone until we were awakened by his cries, and when we rushed to help him, this cruel Witch beat us to the ground and sped far away.

"This morning, I found upon my doorstep a letter. It was from the Witch and said that unless we gave her gold she would return each night and carry away one of our comrades. Help us, Fairy, for this Witch is very powerful."

"Courage, little Man," said the Fairy, "Cho-Cho and I will help you." "Fairy," said Cho-Cho, "I must find this cruel Witch, for if she hurts these little Men, the Children will have no Vegetables to eat, and Children must eat Vegetables. This is what the black mark meant upon the doors," and turning, Cho-Cho walked rapidly away.

Now Cho-Cho had a friend, a Wonderful Dog, who could travel like the wind, and he hurried down the road toward the Dog's house.

Finding the Dog at home, Cho-Cho told him of the little

Men, and added, "I must find this Witch before nightfall, and it is now noon. I cannot travel fast enough, for she lives far away. Will you take me on your back?"

"With pleasure," said the Dog, "but I do not know the way." Leaning forward, Cho-Cho slowly passed his hands before the Dog's eyes. Immediately sight was given to the Dog and he could see far off in the distance the Witch's house and the road that led to it.

"Hurry," said Cho-Cho, seating himself upon the Dog's back, "it grows late."

The great Dog started forward and at each step his pace quickened until his feet scarcely seemed to touch the ground. Faster, faster, and faster he went, and the wind whistled through his long hair, and his beautiful tail waved like a plume. Trees and houses flew by them as they rushed on, and the Dog laughed with glee.

Cho-Cho, clinging on with hands and feet, saw ahead of them a high stone fence. The Dog went over it in a flying leap and landed safely on the other side in a field of grass. Here he began to slacken his pace, for in front of them loomed a dark forest, and only a narrow pathway led through it.

Entering the forest, the Dog was obliged to walk, as the path grew rough and steep, and the underbrush on either side was thick and tangled. At last they came to the mouth of a cave.

"This is the home of the Witch," said Cho-Cho. "We will hide here in the bushes."

Presently they heard a harsh laugh and the ugly Witch came forth from the shadow of the cave. She paused a moment,

     CHO-CHO and THE HEALTH FAIRY Six

dazzled by the sunlight, and Cho-Cho could see clearly the deep scars on her bare ankles, made by chains that had once bound her, and her left arm hung in a sling.

Drawing from his pocket a bright crystal ball, he flashed it directly in the Witch's eyes.

She stood spellbound for several minutes holding one hand to her head, then her body slowly relaxed and she slipped down upon the pathway.

Cho-Cho stepped forth from his hiding place among the bushes, and stood beside the Witch.

She lay quite still as though asleep. "Lie there for two and twenty hours," Cho-Cho said, "and when you awaken your sight shall be so dimmed that never again shall you see clearly—never again shall you molest the Green Vegetables."

Then they went forward into the cave to find the little Vegetable Man. He lay upon the ground, bound hand and foot, trembling with fear.

"Courage, little Man," said Cho-Cho, "we are your friends and have come to take you home," and cutting his bonds, they led him forth from the cave.

"Who are you, Friends?" said the little Man.

"I am Cho-Cho, the Friend of the Children, and this Dog is called Publicity," said Cho-Cho. "We work together for the Health of the Children."

Then mounting the Dog's broad back, they started on their homeward journey.

That night from his Magic Window, Cho-Cho beheld a strange sight, for in the fields and gardens the little Vegetable Men were dancing in the Moonlight, and as they danced, they sang with joy, for the old Witch Ignorance lay helpless in the Forest and they were safe from harm.

  CHO-CHO and THE HEALTH FAIRY Six

O Cho-Cho,
the lovely bird is hurt.

The Lovely Bird

One summer day when the city streets were full of heat and dust, and all the world seemed tired, Cho-Cho's thoughts turned longingly to the country and to the lovely Garden of the little Fairy Health.

Packing his bag and locking the door of his house, Cho-Cho started on a visit to the Fairy.

Within the Fairy's Garden, screened from the road by trees and bushes, was a lovely dell, and in the center of the dell a Fountain, so beautiful that all who saw it paused to admire its sparkling waters and the beauty of its sculptured figure. This figure was of white marble, carved with rare skill into the form of a little child, and from its uplifted hand the waters of the fountain sprang.

Cho-Cho found the Fairy resting in the cool shade and sank into a seat beside her.

"Fairy," said Cho-Cho, "I am grieved about my Children."

"What is wrong, Cho-Cho?" said the little Fairy.

"There are two Imps," said Cho-Cho, "going into all the houses where children live. One is called Dirt, and he leaves upon the Children's hands and faces and in their hair and on their clothes ugly black marks. The other Imp is called

Neglect, and he whispers to the Children not to clean their teeth, or brush their hair, or bathe their bodies. I saw these Imps from my Magic Window, Fairy, and I came to ask your help. What shall we do?"

30"I have a strong friend," said the Fairy, "a Lovely Bird, called Education, and he will go to the Teachers, and they will teach the Children how to be cleanly, and to love the cool pure water."

As she spoke, they heard a noise of wings, and the Lovely Bird fluttered to the ground. Then the Fairy told him of their trouble.

"Courage," said the Bird, "I will go to the Teachers, but my way will be full of peril, for these Imps are powerful and they will try to hold me back. Each day you must watch within this dell. If I am hurt, you will find beside the fountain a Blue-Gray Feather. Then, Cho-Cho, you must hasten to my aid."

As he said this, the Lovely Bird rose into the air, and mounted higher and higher, until he was lost to their view. Day after day Cho-Cho and the Fairy sat beside the fountain watching for the Feather, and after many days had passed, they began to hope that Education had safely reached the Teachers.

Then one day, slowly circling downward from the sky, came a Blue-Gray Feather, and rested at their feet.

"Oh, Cho-Cho," said the Fairy, "the Lovely Bird is hurt," and laying her head upon the fountain's edge, she sobbed with grief and disappointment.

"Courage," said Cho-Cho, "I have a noble ally, a Wonderful Dog, who can travel like the wind. His name is Publicity, and he will help Education. His home is not far distant. Be brave. The Lovely Bird shall soon be free."

Then Cho-Cho hastened to the home of the Dog. Arriving there, he rapped smartly on the door, which was opened 31by the Dog's wife, who said he was just finishing his breakfast—that he would be out immediately.

In a few minutes the Dog appeared. Then Cho-Cho told him of the Lovely Bird.

"I shall be glad to help," said the Wonderful Dog, "but how shall I find the way?"

Taking from his pocket the Blue-Gray Feather, Cho-Cho held it before the Dog's nose. He sniffed it eagerly and then throwing up his head, laughed with glee. "Get up quickly, Cho-Cho," he said, and Cho-Cho sprang upon his back.

The great Dog bounded through the door and out into the road, and with a sharp bark was off like wind.

The Children scurried from the roadside, and people standing in their doorways gazed with wonder as the Dog rushed by. Through villages and towns he went, and everywhere the people ran out to see Publicity pass.

They left the houses far behind, and still the great Dog did not slacken his pace, until they came to desolate fields and a countryside where no trees grew.

On all sides stretched these lonely fields, with no signs of life, except where far away to the right rose the dark outline of a house. A rough path led toward it, and following this road the Dog went forward. As they drew nearer they could see the house was of stone, and had no windows on the lower floor. Up near the roof were narrow windows set deep in the wall. Only a great door in the front, made of iron, gave entrance to the house, and this was tightly locked.

32Sitting on the ground, the Dog took from his neck a

stout collar made of heavy leather and brass, and opening a pocket on the inside of this collar, he took out a Golden Key.

This key fitted the lock, and entering a large room they found the Imps asleep before a fire. As the great door creaked upon its rusty hinges the Imps awakened and sprang to their feet.

"What have you done with the Lovely Bird?" Cho-Cho demanded. "I have seen no bird," said the Imp called Dirt. "You may search this house from dark cellar to dusty garret if you doubt my word."

Cho-Cho turned to his friend the Dog. "Watch here," he said, "and see to it that these Imps do not escape." Then holding his Magic Magnet in his hand he looked about the room. The Magnet turned toward the door at the far corner, and Cho-Cho following the Magnet entered a dark and narrow passage, that seemed to lead on and on. He could not see, but Cho-Cho's stout heart knew no fear for he possessed magic power, that protected him from all evil—so he called to his friend the Moon and asked for help. Mr. Moon had not yet risen, but he sent for his chief Clerk and gave an order, "Send down to my friend Cho-Cho one of our latest flashlights," he said, "one of Golden Light, that will turn the darkest dungeon into the light of day."

So in the shortest possible time Cho-Cho held in his hand a powerful flashlight that showed him every corner of the dark passage, but no matter how carefully he looked he could find no trace of the Lovely Bird.

33Standing there thinking, he heard a faint sound that seemed to come from within the wall, and looking at his Magnet found that it pointed directly opposite.

With his ear at the wall, he heard the sound clearer—then suddenly his eye caught the glint of steel, and he saw a small bright spot about the size of a pea. Cho-Cho pressed the spot and the wall opened showing a tiny room. The Lovely Bird lay on the floor, too weak to fly—so Cho-Cho carried him forth and helped him on the Dog's back.

The wicked Imps knew that their punishment was near and cowered in the corner.

Then Cho-Cho bound the two Imps with strong cords. Standing them back to back he tied their arms together and also their legs, so that they could go neither forward nor backward, and mounting the back of his friend the Wonderful Dog, he started homeward.

They could hear the cries of the Imps far down the roadway, for each one blamed the other with ugly words for what had happened.

When Education felt stronger he flew forward with his Message to the Teachers.

And everywhere the Teachers received him with the deepest interest, and now all over this great country Children are being taught the beauty of cleanliness and the love of fresh air and pure water.

As the Children learn these wholesome health habits, they in turn teach others, and in every home tooth brushes and soap and pure water are to be found, and busy mothers go about their work with cheerful faces, for their Children are healthy and clean and happy.

The company
was all assembled

The Fairy's Party

Neighbors passing the house of the little Fairy Health, one lovely summer day, noticed a most unusual stir and bustle. Large and small packages were continually arriving and the neat little housemaid was kept quite busy opening and closing the door to receive them.

The Fairy, flitting here and there among the flower beds, was accosted by one curious neighbor and asked what it all meant.

With her hands full of flowers the Fairy paused to answer him:

"I am giving a party this afternoon," she said, "to friends from a distance, and we are all very busy."

Cho-Cho, arriving about this time, was told to leave his bag in the house and hurry back to help gather roses.

The curious neighbor departed, and Cho-Cho and the Fairy worked for an hour, gathering flowers and vines, to make the beautiful house more beautiful.

At last it was all finished, and the Fairy hurried upstairs to don her party gown before the guests should arrive.

When she came down the stairs a half hour later, Cho-Cho, waiting in the hallway, held his breath in admiration, for the little Fairy was so lovely that words can scarce describe her. Her gown fell in graceful lines about her slender figure—neck and arms were bare, and her flower-like face crowned with its shining hair was radiant with joy. Forget-me-nots were twined among her curls, and she carried a 36bunch of them in her shapely hands. No jewels adorned the Fairy, but in every way she expressed simplicity and grace.

Cho-Cho, coming forward, dropped lightly on one knee, and taking the Fairy's hand, raised it to his lips.

"You are wonderful," he said.

"You like my gown, Cho-Cho?" she questioned, and smiled upon him, for these two were old and tried friends.

A noise from without told of the advent of a guest, and Health went forward to greet the visitor.

It proved to be the Persian Cat, looking quite handsome in a soft-gray hat, which he gracefully doffed to the Fairy, and he carried a gold-headed cane.

One could well imagine him a great favorite with the ladies, for he was indeed a finished dandy.

"You rival your flowers in beauty, Fairy," he said, as he took her hand.

At the noise of the garden gate closing, they looked up to behold the Wonderful Dog and his wife coming toward them.

The Wonderful Dog had on a smart new collar, and came forward with dignity to present his wife to the Fairy, for they had never met.

Mrs. Dog was a fluffy little thing, who seemed really to

care more about her new dress and the latest style than any other subject.

The next arrival was the little Boy from the Farm. He came timidly toward the group, looking rather frightened, but when he spied his old friend, Cho-Cho, all his fears vanished and he smiled with pleasure.

37They were busily chatting in the Rose Arbor, when the little Vegetable Men came softly in and stood beside the Fairy.

She welcomed them with kindness, for these were modest little people and felt rather strange among the handsome company.

With a whirr of wings and a flash of color, the Lovely Bird and his brother Rumor were among them and congratulated the Fairy on the perfect weather she was having for her Fête.

The company were all assembled now except the Red Brown Squirrel, and the Fairy asked if anyone had seen him on the high-road as they came hither. But no one had heard of him, although the Persian Cat had come from that direction.

An hour slipped by. The Fairy was growing anxious and Cho-Cho repeatedly looked at his watch.

At last he said:

"With your permission, Fairy, I will go look for the Red Brown Squirrel. He was my friend and I greatly fear some evil has befallen him."

"I, too, will go," said the Cat, "there are many dangers upon the high-road, and a comrade may be needed."

"I am with you," said the Dog. "Lead on, Cho-Cho."

"Friends," said the Persian Cat, "I believe I can find the Red Brown Squirrel. Between his home and the Fairy's garden there lives an evil imp, called Jealousy. I passed him today as I journeyed hither and he scowled upon me with a look of rage. He was afraid to attack me, but the 38Squirrel is small and not a match for this cruel imp, and has doubtless fallen a victim to his malice."

"Hasten, hasten," said Cho-Cho, and passing through the gate he started briskly toward the Squirrel's home.

The Cat and the Dog followed and all three were soon lost to the view of the anxious company in the Fairy's garden.

The friends covered the ground rapidly and were nearing the home of the Red Brown Squirrel, when Cho-Cho's sharp eyes spied a half-eaten nut lying in the roadway.

There were no trees near, and they knew that it must have been dropped by their friend.

Looking eagerly upon the ground, they discovered the tiny footprints of the Squirrel and the larger ones of the flat-footed imp, leading into a field of tall grass.

Here the Cat went forward, for his sharp eyes could distinguish the footprints with great ease. Following these signs they crossed the field and came out upon an unused road that sloped downward, until they found themselves beside a deep river which seemed impossible to pass.

"Get upon my back," said the Wonderful Dog, "the River is my comrade, it will not harm you."

With ease and confidence he swam forward, and carried them to safety on the further bank.

Cho-Cho and the Persian Cat stepped from the Dog's back and turned to thank him, when from behind a large rock, the ugly imp darted out and sprang toward Cho-Cho, trying to push him into the river. But the Cat, catching the imp by the neck, held him firmly, and he was powerless to do aught but scream.

39Binding him fast they went behind the great rock and found the Red Brown Squirrel in chains.

The Cat set him free and the friendly Squirrel stood up before them brave and unhurt.

Then they hurried back to the Fairy and were received with relief and pleasure.

And now, the Fairy with the Wonderful Dog leads the way to the dining-room. The Persian Cat gracefully offers his arm to little Mrs. Dog. Cho-Cho and the Boy come hand in hand, followed by the Lovely Bird and Mr. Beet. The Red Brown Squirrel is telling the story of his adventure to Mr. Onion, and Rumor and Mr. Carrot bring up the rear.

The dining-room is a mass of roses and smilax, and in the center, a table full of all the delicious things that children like.

Mrs. Dog remarks that the decorations are lovely, and the Persian Cat replies that the ladies are more beautiful than the flowers.

The little Fairy flits here and there among her guests, seeing, with charming courtesy, that all their wants are well supplied, and when at last they can eat no more, Cho-Cho rises, and with a glass of sparkling lemonade proposes a toast:

"To our charming hostess, the Fairy Health."

With a right good will the company drink the toast, then led by the Persian Cat they leave the house and with laughter and jest pass by lovely garden paths out to the fountain—and so the fun goes on, ending at last with a dance in the dell, and joy and happiness in every heart.